The Incredible Holiday Activity Book

ANGELA WILKES

DORLING KINDERSLEY
London • New York • Stuttgart • Moscow

A Dorling Kindersley Book

Art Editor   Cheryl Telfer
Editor   Victoria Edgley
Photographer   Dave King

Managing Editor   Jane Yorke
Managing Art Editor   Chris Scollen
Production   Josie Alabaster
DTP Designer   Almudena Díaz

First published in Great Britain in 1997
by Dorling Kindersley Limited
9 Henrietta Street, London WC2E 8PS
Reprinted 1997

Visit us on the World Wide Web at http://www.dk.com

A CIP catalogue record for this book
is available from the British Library.

ISBN: 0-7513-5506-2

Colour reproduction by Bright Arts, Hong Kong
Printed and bound in Italy by A. Montadori Editore, Verona

Picture credits: The Image Bank/ Sumo; 3crb, 43cl, 45tl.

Dorling Kindersley would like to thank Alison Dunne
for jacket design and Lissa Martin from
World's End Nurseries. Dorling Kindersley would also
like to thank the following models for appearing
in this book: Maria Beckworth, Sarah Bennett,
Gina Caffrey, Jay Davis, Candy Day, Lorna Holmes,
Tebedge Ricketts, and Elizabeth Workman.

CONTENTS

OUTDOOR ACTIVITIES

INTRODUCTION

Whether you go away for your holiday or stay at home, this book is full of inspiring ideas for great things to make and do using everyday materials. Before you start, collect your holiday souvenirs and some basic equipment. Below you can see some useful things to save. When you have finished a project, remember to put everything away and clean up any mess you have made.

Things to collect

Spiral-bound notebook

Leaves

Buttons

Sea glass

Shells

Paper

Sketchbook

Rope

Coins

Disposable pocket camera

String

Map

Ticket

Coloured pencils

Keeping record

Notebooks and small sketchbooks are useful for making notes and quick sketches of interesting things that you see. Carry a pocket camera so that you can take photos for souvenirs.

Treasures and souvenirs

Collect as many interesting things as you can find on your holiday. Shells, pebbles, driftwood, dried leaves, tickets, coins, and maps will form the basis of many of your projects.

Warning symbols

Look out for the red warning signs in the step-by-step instructions of some projects.

The warning symbol
You will see this sign when sharp tools are used. Always ask an adult to help you.

Seeing stars

At the top of each page you will find a star symbol that tells you how long the most difficult project on each page takes.

One star
☆ Project takes an hour or less to complete.

Two stars
☆☆ Project takes an afternoon to complete.

Three stars
☆☆☆ Project takes a day or more to complete.

Coloured tape

Tissue paper

Paintbrushes

Pencil

Pens

Strong glue

Glue stick

Tape-measure

Scissors   *Craft knife*   *Ruler*   *PVA glue*

Ribbons

Coloured fabric

Craft materials

The more craft materials you have, the more choice you will have for your projects. Collect different colours and types of paper and card. Keep them in a folder so they stay flat. You will also need various sorts of glue, sticky tape, paints, pencils, and pens. Start a bag of leftover pieces of fabric and ribbons and put together a small sewing kit with a tape-measure, scissors, needles, and pins.

FLUTTERING FLAGS

Even the humblest sandcastle can look truly magnificent with its own special flag, so get out your paints and make an array of flags before going to the beach. Try making a colourful pennant to hang at the beach or in your garden.

EQUIPMENT

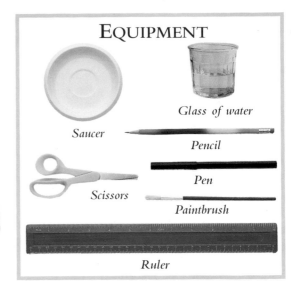

Saucer

Glass of water

Pencil

Scissors

Pen

Paintbrush

Ruler

You will need

White and coloured card

Sticky tape

Plastic drinking straws and swizzle sticks

String

Coloured plastic bags

Gummed stars and spots

Glue stick

Poster paints

Strong glue

Making a pennant

1 Using a pen and ruler, draw lots of triangles the same size on different coloured pieces of plastic. Then carefully cut out the triangles.

2 Fold the top of each triangle over a long piece of string and tape it in place. Space the triangles out along the string.

Making castle flags

1 Draw different shaped flags on card and cut them out. Paint designs on each one and stick stars or spots on some of the flags.

2 Cut out triangular shaped flags and fold them several times. Then glue the back edge of each flag to a plastic drinking straw or swizzle stick.

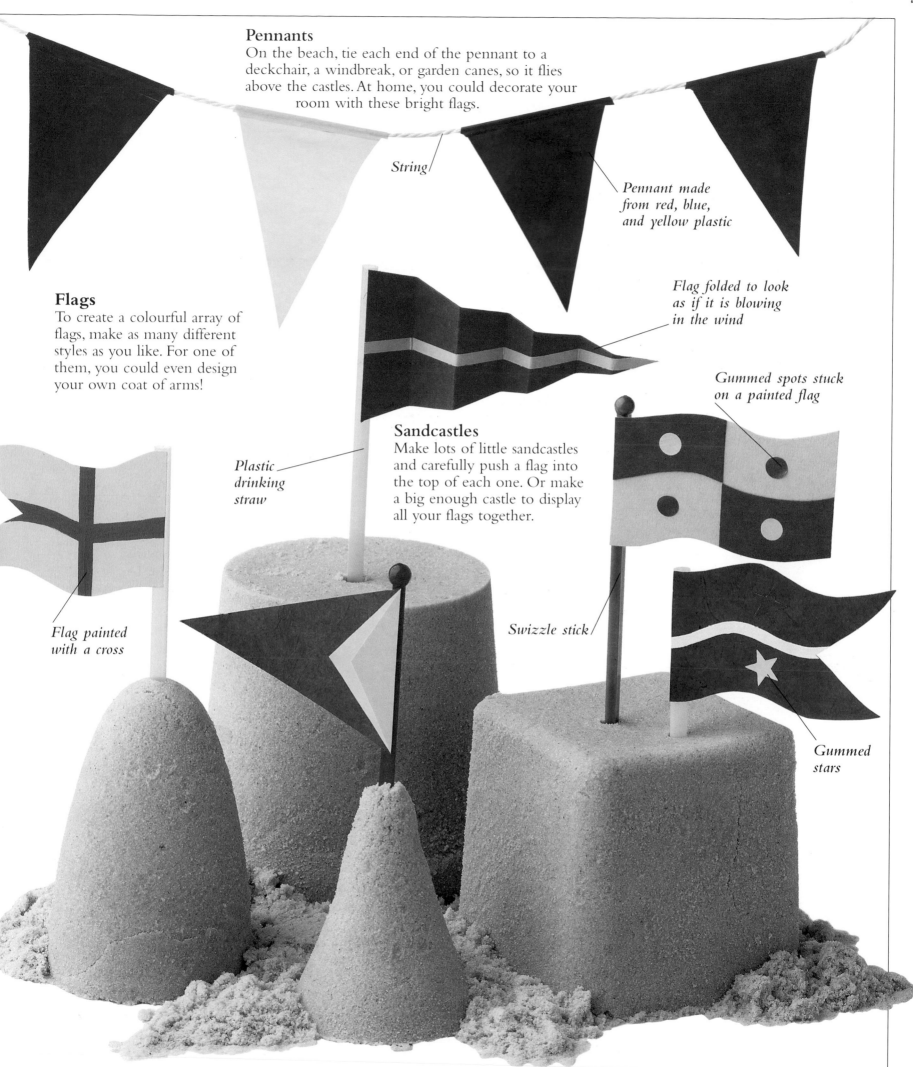

Pennants

On the beach, tie each end of the pennant to a deckchair, a windbreak, or garden canes, so it flies above the castles. At home, you could decorate your room with these bright flags.

String

Pennant made from red, blue, and yellow plastic

Flag folded to look as if it is blowing in the wind

Flags

To create a colourful array of flags, make as many different styles as you like. For one of them, you could even design your own coat of arms!

Gummed spots stuck on a painted flag

Plastic drinking straw

Sandcastles

Make lots of little sandcastles and carefully push a flag into the top of each one. Or make a big enough castle to display all your flags together.

Flag painted with a cross

Swizzle stick

Gummed stars

GOING FISHING

Here you can find out how to make a simple fishing rod and drop net for your fishing expeditions. Use the rod to catch fish from a riverbank or from a pier. A drop net is good for catching crabs and other small shellfish from rock pools.

You will need

For the rod

Cork

Garden cane 2 m long

Coloured tape

For the drop net

Cubes of bread and cheese for bait

Embroidery hoops 35 cm across

3 m thick thread or nylon fishing line

Enamel paint

For a lure

4 m thick cord

Coloured thread

Bead   *Paper clip*

Stone

Thread

Coloured feathers

50 cm x 100 cm fine net or mesh

EQUIPMENT

Darning needle

Scissors   *Tape-measure*

Needle

Paintbrush

Pins

Making the drop net

1 Fold the net in half (50 cm x 50 cm). Pin along two sides, leaving one side open. Sew★ along the pinned sides, about 1 cm in from the edge.

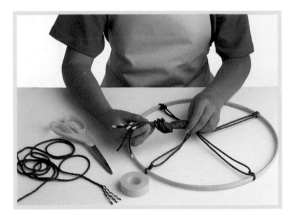

2 To make a handle, cut four pieces of cord each 1 m long. Tie them to the outside embroidery hoop, and then tie the loose ends together.

3 Tie a stone at the bottom of the net. Fold the top of the net over the inside hoop and ask an adult to help fit the other hoop over it.

Making the rod

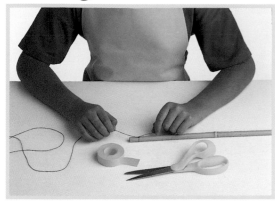

1 Tie one end of the thread to one end of the cane. Wind the thread around the cane several times and hold it in place with coloured tape.

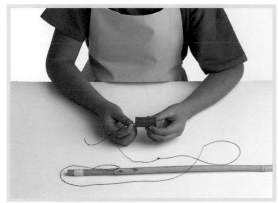

2 Make a hole through a cork with a needle. Paint it and let it dry. Knot the thread 1 m from the end, slip on the cork and tie another knot.

3 Open out a paper clip into a hook and bind feathers to the centre with thread. Push a bead on the top end and bend the wire in.

Going for the catch

Hook bait, such as cheese, bread, or bacon rind on your fishing line, or hang it from the drop net's handle. Now just wait for a catch!

Feathered lure

Cheese bait on hook

Knot in the line

Float made from a painted cork

Using the rod

When you have a catch, the float will bob up and down. Pull the line in carefully to see what you have caught, or scoop up fish attracted to the bait with a net.

Lures

Lures like this are meant to look like flies and attract fish. Make a few so you have some spares.

Bead

Hook

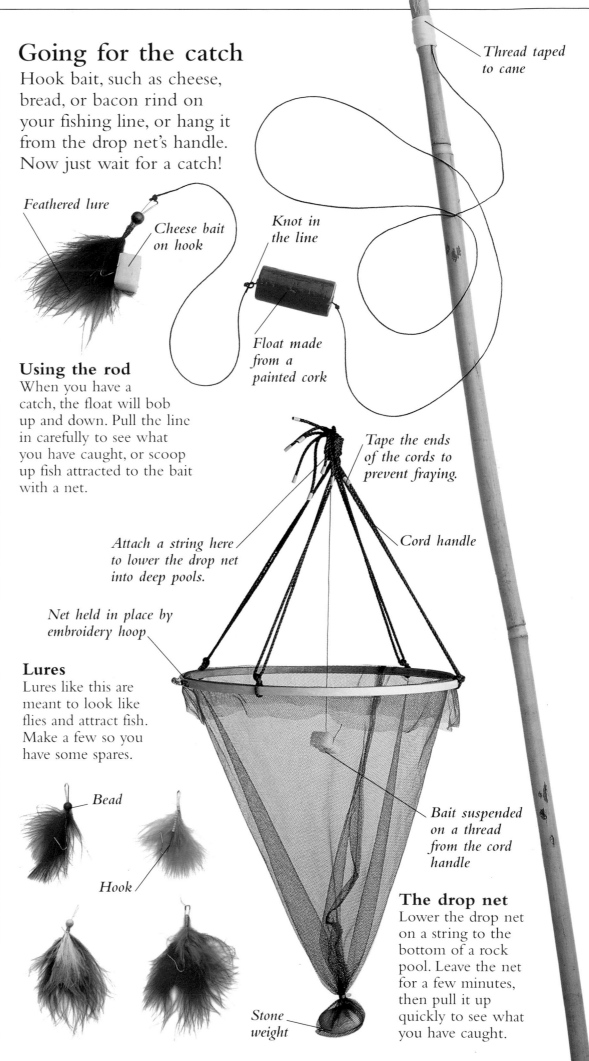

Thread taped to cane

Tape the ends of the cords to prevent fraying.

Attach a string here to lower the drop net into deep pools.

Cord handle

Net held in place by embroidery hoop

Bait suspended on a thread from the cord handle

The drop net

Lower the drop net on a string to the bottom of a rock pool. Leave the net for a few minutes, then pull it up quickly to see what you have caught.

Stone weight

GARDEN WATCH

To attract wildlife into your garden, set up some mini-habitats. Here and over the page you can find out how to make a bee and butterfly garden, build a log pile habitat, set up insect traps, and keep minibeast records in a nature notebook and chart. Start the bee and butterfly garden in spring so you can watch it grow and attract insects over the summer months.

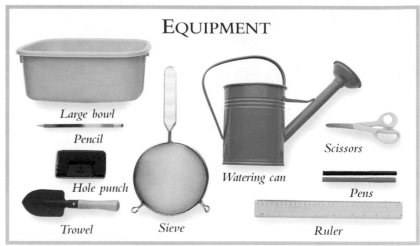

EQUIPMENT

Large bowl

Pencil

Hole punch

Trowel

Sieve

Watering can

Scissors

Pens

Ruler

You will need

For the log pile habitat

Large brick

Soil

Bark and twigs

Fern

Primula

Logs

Ivy

For the insect traps

Small tile

Miniature flowerpot

Grapefruit

Potato

Bacon rind and bread

For the bee and butterfly garden

Four small stones

Yogurt pot

Dry leaves

Lavender

For the chart and notebook

Spiral-bound notebook

Sticky tape

Strong glue

Thyme

Cord

Coloured pencils

Bug bottle

Green, white, and yellow card

Thin ribbon

Small leaves

Sunflower seeds

Flowerpot and saucer

Log pile habitat

1 You can make this in a corner of the garden, or in a window box. Stack and arrange some logs, bricks, and bark on the soil.

2 Plant the ivy, fern, primula, and any other plants to create a natural environment. Fill in empty areas with dead leaves and small twigs.

3 To make a pitfall trap, scoop out a hole in the ground and sink the yogurt pot into it. Drop some bacon rinds into the pot as bait.

4 Lay the four stones around the top of the yogurt pot, as shown. Place a small tile on top of the stones so that it is raised above the pot rim.

5 To make hideaways for insects and other creepy crawlies, stuff flowerpots with dead leaves. Lay the pots on their sides.

6 For extra traps, cut a grapefruit in half, scoop out the middle, and put cubes of bread in it. Do the same with a potato. Place it in the habitat.

Bee and butterfly garden

1 To repot a plant, put some soil in the bottom of a new, larger pot. Gently remove the plant and soil from its old pot, as shown.

2 Lower the plant into the new flowerpot, then fill the pot with soil. Press the soil down firmly around the plant and water it well.

3 For the sunflowers, fill a pot with soil. Push five sunflower seeds into the soil about 1 cm deep. Water the soil and keep it well watered.

NATURE SURVEY

Nature chart

Decorate some card and make a chart by drawing grids on some paper. With the hole punch, make a hole and attach the grids to the card with cord.

Studying minibeasts

1 Try sifting some soil and leaves from the log pile area into a large bowl. How many types of minibeast can you find left in the sieve?

2 Put any creatures you find in the bug bottle to study them. Draw them accurately and then put them back where you found them.

Wildlife in the garden

Keep a regular watch on the log pile habitat and bee and butterfly garden to see how many creatures are attracted to them. Practise making quick sketches of creatures you find. To find out more about the minibeasts, you could look them up in a reference book.

Nature chart

Week 1				
(beetle)				✓
(beetle)			✓	
(slug)	✓			
(ant)		✓		
(woodlouse)				
(snail)	✓		✓	

Grids

Nature notebook
Make sketches of insects in your notebook. Start with three circles for the head, thorax, and abdomen. Then add legs, wings or wing cases, antennae, and any special features.

Ivy

Insect trap chart
Draw the traps at the top of the chart and the creatures you find on the left hand side. Use the chart to record those creatures you have found in the insect traps by ticking the correct box. You could add the time and date that you found the insects.

Log pile habitat
Carefully lift logs and bricks and look under dead leaves to find out which creatures have moved into your log pile. Keep a regular check on the insect traps and make a note of what you find there. Make sure you release any minibeasts caught in the traps.

Large brick

Head

Abdomen

Garden minibeasts

Thorax

Bee and butterfly garden
Plant this garden in spring. Place the
pots in a sunny spot and water them to
keep the soil damp. Butterflies and bees
are attracted to most plants with flowers,
so you could use other flowering plants
for the garden instead.

Bee

Butterfly

Primula

Thyme

Sunflowers

Lavender

Fern

Twigs

Potato trap

Log

Grapefruit trap

Pitfall trap

Flowerpot
hideaway

13

MINIATURE GARDEN

Here and on the next page you can find out how to create a real miniature garden of your own, complete with its own paving and garden furniture. Below are a selection of some plants you could use, but if you can't find these, use similar plants. For an outdoor garden, the best plants to use are miniatures with tiny flowers and small leaves.

Here and on the next page you can find out how to create a real miniature garden of your own

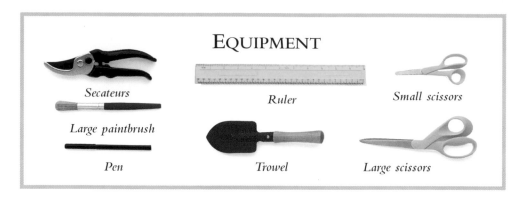

EQUIPMENT

Secateurs

Large paintbrush

Pen

Ruler

Trowel

Small scissors

Large scissors

You will need

For the garden furniture

For the garden

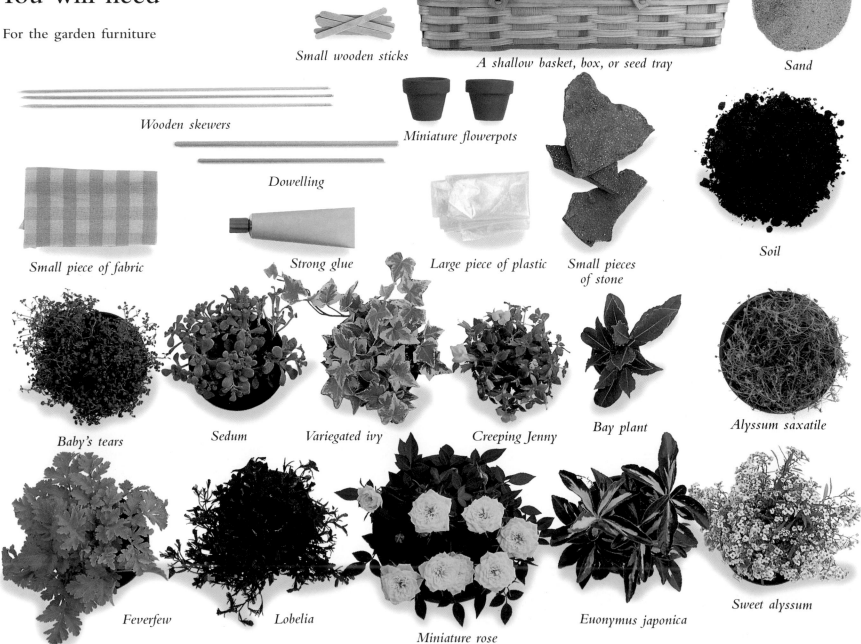

Small wooden sticks

A shallow basket, box, or seed tray

Sand

Wooden skewers

Miniature flowerpots

Dowelling

Soil

Small piece of fabric

Strong glue

Large piece of plastic

Small pieces of stone

Baby's tears

Sedum

Variegated ivy

Creeping Jenny

Bay plant

Alyssum saxatile

Feverfew

Lobelia

Miniature rose

Euonymus japonica

Sweet alyssum

Making the deckchair

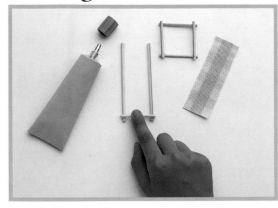

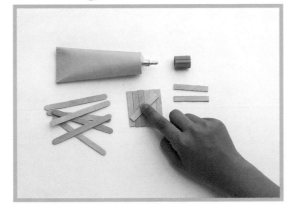

1 Cut★ four 5 cm sticks from a wooden skewer and glue into a square. Glue a 5 cm stick to the end of two sticks 10 cm long, as shown.

2 Glue the square to the sides of the long sticks to make a deckchair frame. Attach a strip of fabric 4 cm x 10 cm in place to make a seat.

Making the trellis

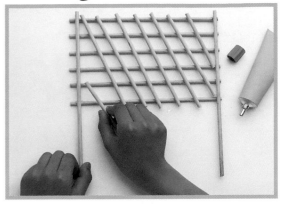

Glue six sticks of dowelling 20 cm long to two sticks 22 cm long. Cut★ six 13 cm sticks and two 8 cm sticks. Glue diagonally on to the cross sticks.

Making the pyramid

Making the table

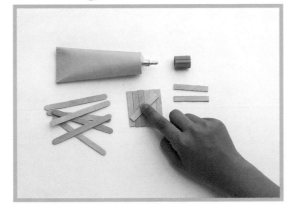

To make a pyramid, join the ends of three pieces of dowelling, 30 cm long. Stick short pieces of dowelling of varying length across them.

1 Cut★ seven pieces of stick 6 cm long. Put six sticks together for a table top and glue the last stick across them, to hold them together.

2 For legs, glue four 5 cm pieces of dowelling to each end of two 5 cm pieces of wooden stick. Glue the sticks to the table top, as shown.

Making the garden

1 Line the basket with some plastic and cut small holes for drainage. Using the trowel, fill the basket about two-thirds full with the soil.

2 Now plan out your garden. Leave the plants in their containers and arrange them in the basket to see where they look best.

3 Decide where to position the trellis, path, and patio. Make a patio and path by laying large and small stones on the soil.

★Ask an adult to cut dowelling, wooden sticks, and skewers for you using the secateurs.

A SMALL WORLD
Planting the garden

1 Remove the plants from the pots and plant any tall plants. Put the trellis and pyramid in place. Add ivy by the trellis and a rose in the pyramid.

A secret garden
The finished garden is a real world in miniature, with winding paths and shady spots for tables or deckchairs. Stand the garden outside in a bright spot and water it well. It is important to care for your garden and look after your plants all year round. Trim the plants if they get too overgrown, and snip off any dead leaves or flowers. Keep the soil moist by spraying it with water from a spray bottle.

Feverfew

Steps created by laying stones on top of each other

Lobelia

Snip off any dead flower-heads to encourage the plants to keep flowering.

2 To make a lawn, plant creeping, low-growing plants, such as Baby's tears. Carefully press the plants in place.

3 Fill in all the gaps in the garden with small, brightly-coloured, flowering plants. Lobelia and Sweet alyssum make good fillers.

4 Sprinkle sand over the patio and paths. Use a wide paintbrush to brush the sand into the cracks between the stones.

5 Add the garden furniture. Fill the miniature flowerpots with small flowers or herb plants and position them in the garden.

Miniature rose
entwined through
pyramid

Ivy woven
through trellis

Miniature
bay plant
in a pot

Patio area

Sedum

Sand brushed
between stones

Path made of
small stones

Cane basket lined
with plastic and
filled with soil

TOP TO TOE

With a little imagination you can transform ordinary straw hats, baseball caps, and canvas shoes into personalized works of art, which are fun to decorate as well as wear. Gather together colourful beads, buttons, and other odds and ends before you start.

EQUIPMENT

Pencil

Darning needle

Scissors

You will need

For the shoes

For the cap

For the sunhat

Baseball cap

Strong glue

Plain canvas shoes

Straw sunhat

Sticky tape

Plastic bag ties

Coloured buttons

Coloured buttons

Washers

Coloured beads

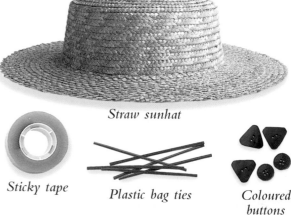

Tubes of all-surface fabric paint *

Coloured tissue paper

Straw sunhat

1 Cut large and small flowers out of red and purple tissue paper. Roll up strips of purple tissue. Secure with tape and snip a fringe.

2 Glue together several flower shapes. Thread a button on a tie and twist the end to secure it. Pull the tie through a purple roll.

3 Push a tie through the centre of a flower. Thread the needle with the tie and attach it to the crown of the hat. Bend the tie back, to secure it.

Available from large department stores or craft shops.

Canvas shoes

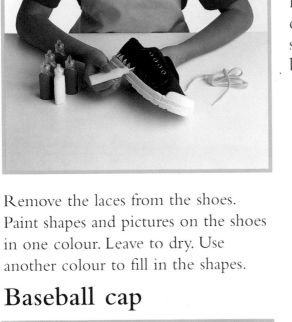

Remove the laces from the shoes. Paint shapes and pictures on the shoes in one colour. Leave to dry. Use another colour to fill in the shapes.

Baseball cap

Glue buttons, beads, and washers to the cap in a pattern. Stick smaller buttons and beads on top of larger ones to add more detail.

Stepping out

Copy these decorative ideas or experiment with your own. For example, you could try covering a straw hat or canvas shoes with buttons and a baseball cap with fabric paints.

Nautical shoes

These canvas shoes have a seaside theme, with pictures of a boat, anchor, and lifebuoy.

Bright yellow laces add a splash of colour.

Wavy water-line

Button caps

Use brightly coloured beads and buttons in as many different shapes as you can find to decorate your cap and create patterns.

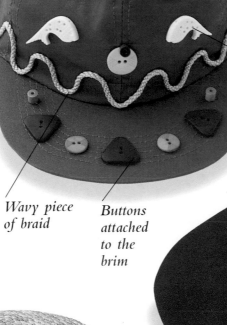

Fish-shaped buttons

Wavy piece of braid

Buttons attached to the brim

Washer and bead on top of a button

Fringed purple tissue paper with a button in the centre

Red flower petals

Purple flowers made in the same way as the red flowers

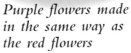

Floral sunhat

Fasten three large red flowers to the front of the hat, and smaller, purple flowers around the crown.

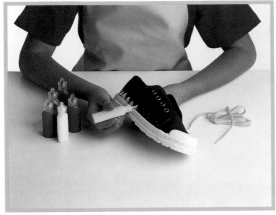

DECORATING T-SHIRTS

You can transform plain T-shirts with amazing designs by painting, printing, stencilling, or tie-dying them. Use white, or light-coloured T-shirts for the best results and choose fabric paints in strong, contrasting colours. It is a good idea to draw a clear design for each T-shirt before you start. Turn the page to see what great works of art you can produce in an afternoon.

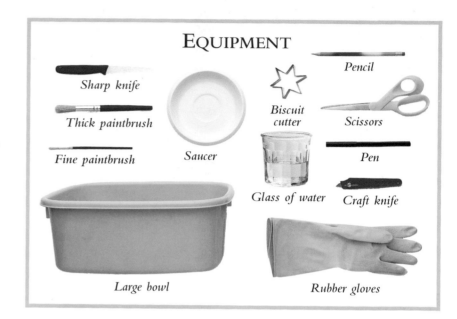

EQUIPMENT

Sharp knife

Thick paintbrush

Fine paintbrush

Saucer

Biscuit cutter

Glass of water

Pencil

Scissors

Pen

Craft knife

Large bowl

Rubber gloves

You will need

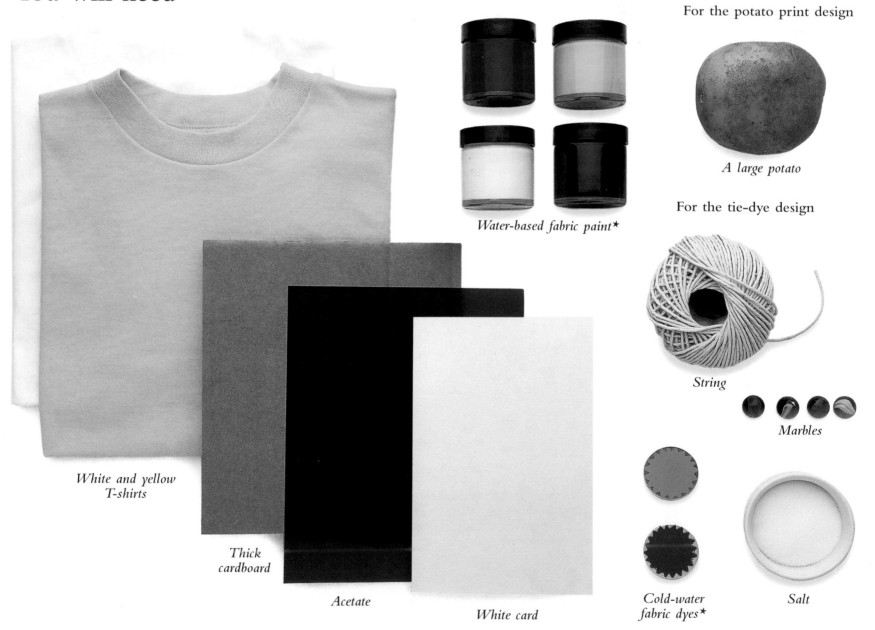

White and yellow T-shirts

Thick cardboard

Acetate

White card

Water-based fabric paint★

For the potato print design

A large potato

For the tie-dye design

String

Marbles

Cold-water fabric dyes★

Salt

★Available from large department stores or craft shops.

Stencilled T-shirt

1 Draw shapes for stencils on the acetate. Lay the acetate on thick card and ask an adult to cut the stencils out with a craft knife.

2 Lay a stencil flat on the T-shirt. Decide which colour paint to use, then dab it all over the cut-out stencil with a paintbrush.

3 Carefully lift the stencil off the T-shirt, so you do not smudge the paint. Continue using other stencils and different colours. Leave to dry.

Hand-painted T-shirt

1 Draw a design on some white card to the size you want for your T-shirt. Use a dark pen and keep the design bold and simple.

2 Slip the card inside the T-shirt so the design is where you want it. Paint over the outline of the design in a light coloured fabric paint.

3 Paint in the main colour of the design and let it dry. Then add the details in other colours, keeping the paint as thick as you can.

Potato print T-shirt

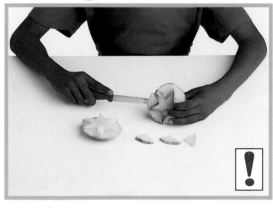

1 Slice a potato in half. Press a star-shaped biscuit cutter into each half of the potato. Then carefully cut away the potato around the cutter.

2 Mix some thick paint in a saucer. Cover the potato star with a thick coat of paint, then firmly press it down in position on the T-shirt.

3 Lift the potato off carefully. Use the other half of the potato to print another colour. Repaint the potatoes each time you use them.

T-SHIRTS ON SHOW

The finished T-shirts are bold and colourful. Let the paint or dye on each T-shirt dry and then ask an adult to help you iron them. You can copy the designs shown here, or try experimenting with pictures and patterns of your own.

Tie-dyed T-shirts

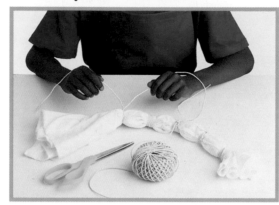

1 To make a stripy T-shirt, roll up a white T-shirt tightly. Tie long pieces of string securely around the T-shirt at 10 cm intervals.

2 For a circular design, tie a marble in the middle of the T-shirt's front and in each sleeve. Tie string at 5 cm intervals from each marble.

A white T-shirt tie-dyed in red with marbles and string creates a circular effect.

Red and yellow star-shaped potato prints

An all over design with hand-painted sunflowers

Circular T-shirt

Starry T-shirt

Sunflower T-shirt

3 Wearing rubber gloves, mix the cold-water dye in a bowl. Follow the instructions on the packet and add the salt. Soak the T-shirt in the dye.

4 After one hour, take the T-shirt out of the dye and wring it well. Rinse the T-shirt under cold water until the water runs clean.

5 Very carefully cut the string tied around the T-shirt and remove all the ties and marbles. Hang the T-shirt up to dry, then iron it.

Large hand-painted picture

A white T-shirt tie-dyed in blue with string, creates these stripes.

Stencilled fish and seashells around the top and bottom

Cockerel T-shirt

Stripy T-shirt

Seaside T-shirt

SUMMER COOLERS

What's better on a hot summer's day than a cool, refreshing drink? Here are three tasty recipes for you to try. The sunset punch and fruit cooler can be made in minutes, and both make enough for two people. The fresh lemonade needs to be prepared one day in advance before drinking. This recipe makes enough for four thirsty people.

You will need

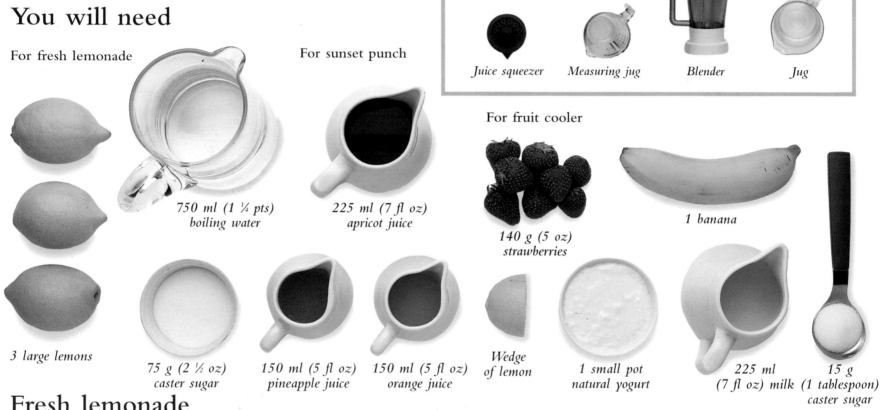

EQUIPMENT

Chopping board

Sieve

Large bowl

Potato peeler

Large spoon

Sharp knife

Juice squeezer

Measuring jug

Blender

Jug

For fresh lemonade

750 ml (1 ¼ pts)
boiling water

For sunset punch

225 ml (7 fl oz)
apricot juice

For fruit cooler

140 g (5 oz)
strawberries

1 banana

3 large lemons

75 g (2 ½ oz)
caster sugar

150 ml (5 fl oz)
pineapple juice

150 ml (5 fl oz)
orange juice

Wedge
of lemon

1 small pot
natural yogurt

225 ml
(7 fl oz) milk

15 g
(1 tablespoon)
caster sugar

Fresh lemonade

1 Wash the lemons. With the peeler remove the peel from two lemons into a bowl. Trim off any white pieces of pith you find on the peel.

2 Cut all three lemons in half and squeeze their juice into the bowl. Add the sugar, then carefully stir in the boiling water.

3 Leave the lemonade in a cool place overnight. Then strain the mixture through a sieve into a jug, ready to serve.

Fruit cooler

Sunset punch

1 Peel the banana. Slice and put it into the blender. Squeeze a little lemon juice on top. Wash the strawberries and chop off the stalks.

2 Put the yogurt into the blender with the bananas, strawberries, milk, and sugar. Blend for about a minute, until frothy. Serve into a glass.

Pour the orange juice, pineapple juice, and apricot juice into a jug and mix them together well with a large spoon. Chill before serving.

Fruity refreshers

Pour the drinks into tall glasses. Add ice cubes made from fruit juice or with pieces of fruit set into them, and serve with sliced fruit and coloured drinking straws.

Fruit cooler

Strawberry slotted on to the edge of the glass

Sunset punch

Add ice cubes made from cranberry juice, for a sunset glow.

Novelty drinking straw

Fresh lemonade

Half a strawberry frozen into an ice cube

Cut a slit to the middle of each orange and lemon slice and slot them on to the glass.

ALL IN A POCKET

Here you can find out how to make a cook's apron, a gardener's apron, a tool kit, and an organiser. Copy the patterns at the bottom of the page using the measurements shown. Use running stitch★ to sew the aprons. Turn the page to see the final results.

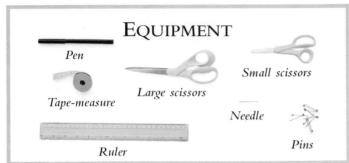

EQUIPMENT

Pen

Tape-measure

Large scissors

Small scissors

Needle

Ruler

Pins

You will need

Dowelling for organiser

Graph paper

Thread to match your fabric

Coloured curtain fabric

2 m of ribbon for each project

Making the patterns

Copy the aprons and pocket patterns below on to graph paper using the measurements shown and cut them out. Adapt the patterns to fit you if they are too big or small. Pin the pattern pieces you need to the fabric, making sure that they are straight. Cut the fabric out, then remove the pattern pieces.

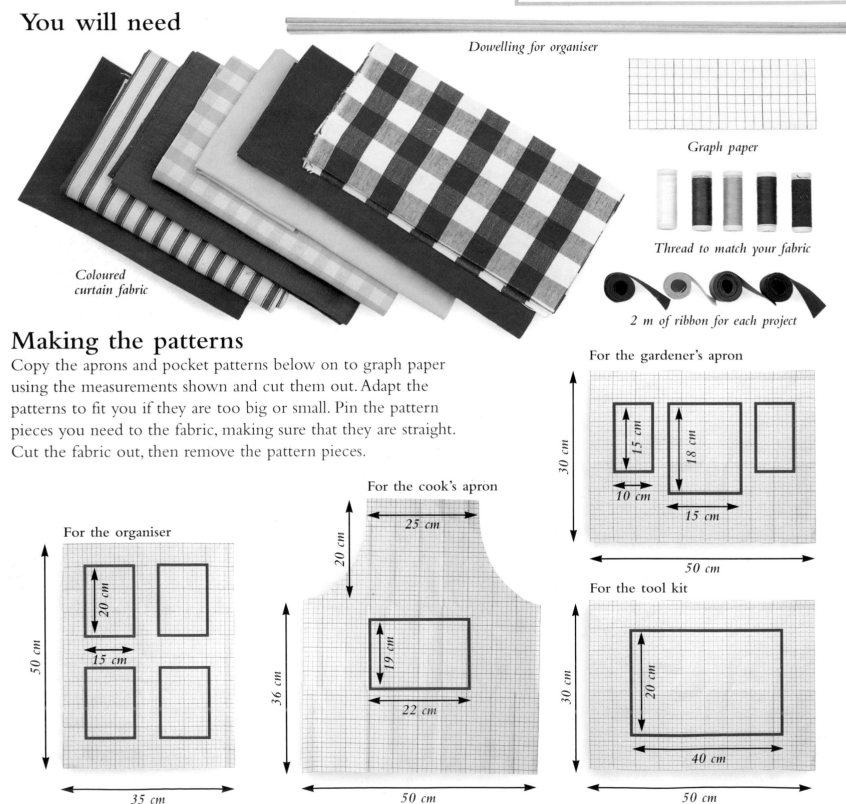

For the gardener's apron

30 cm

15 cm

18 cm

10 cm

15 cm

50 cm

For the organiser

50 cm

20 cm

15 cm

35 cm

For the cook's apron

25 cm

20 cm

19 cm

22 cm

36 cm

50 cm

For the tool kit

30 cm

20 cm

40 cm

50 cm

*Running stitch is straight, little stitches woven in and out of the fabric.

Making the cook's apron

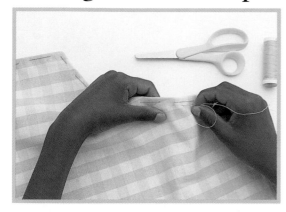

1 To make a neat hem, fold the apron material over 1 cm at the edge and fold it again. Tack★ the edge in place then sew it in running stitch.

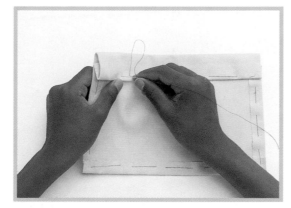

2 Tack a 1 cm hem around the sides and bottom of the pocket. Tack and sew a hem 1.5 cm deep at the top edge of the pocket.

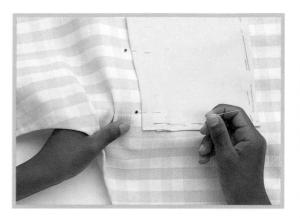

3 Pin the pocket to the centre of the apron. Tack the pocket in place then sew it in running stitch along the bottom and sides.

Making the organiser

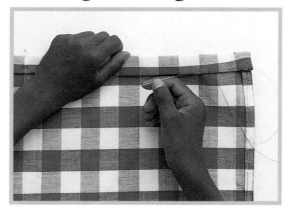

1 Tack and sew a 1 cm hem down the long sides of the fabric. Tack and sew a 2 cm hem at the top and bottom of the rectangle.

4 Tack a line across the middle of the pocket to divide it in two. Using the tacking as a guide, sew a straight line across the pocket.

5 Cut a ribbon 56 cm long for the apron top and two ribbons 50 cm long for each side. Fold over the ends and sew them to the apron back.

Making the tool kit

2 Make the pockets as in step 2 above. Pin, tack, and sew them to the fabric. Cut a ribbon 40 cm long and sew it to the top of the organiser.

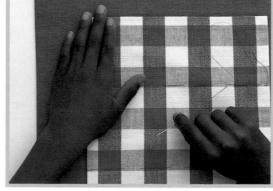

1 Sew the edges of the kit. Tack and sew on the pocket, as for the cook's apron. To divide up the pocket, sew two lines 10 cm from each side.

2 Cut four 50 cm lengths of ribbon. Sew two ribbons on the back of the top right corner and the other two to the bottom right corner.

To tack, sew in big stitches using contrasting thread. Remove the tacking stitches when you have done the running stitch.

KITS AND APRONS
Making the gardener's apron

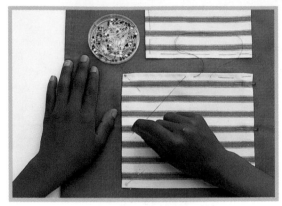

1 Hem the edges of the apron and make the pockets as for the cook's apron. Pin, tack, and sew the pockets to the apron 7 cm from the top edge.

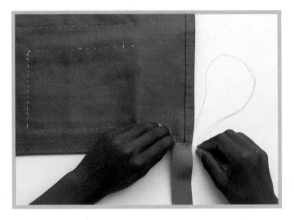

2 Cut two pieces of ribbon 50 cm long. Turn in the edges and sew one ribbon to each top edge of the apron, at the back of the fabric.

Organiser
Hang the organiser on your bedroom wall or above a desk. Use it to hold all your pens and store other odds and ends.

Hang the organiser up by the ribbon loop.

To make the organiser hang correctly, insert the dowelling into the 2 cm hems at the top and bottom.

Individual pockets

Pocket in a contrasting colour to checked fabric

Finished products
Choose fabrics in bold colours or patterns for the kits and aprons. Checks and stripes look good with plain colours and are easy to sew as you can use them as guidelines for stitching.

Gardener's apron
Tuck your gardening tools, gloves, and packets of seeds away in these practical pockets. Roll up the apron when you have finished using it.

Two smaller pockets at each side of a large pocket

Tool kit
Keep your work area tidy by putting your tools, screws, and nails together in the divided pockets of the tool kit. Roll the kit up, starting from the end without the ties. Fasten the kit by tying the four ties at the end around the kit.

Two ties sewn to one side at the top

Two ties sewn at the bottom of the kit

Pocket divided into three by two lines of stitching

Try the apron patterns against you before cutting them out and make them longer or wider if you want.

Tie sewn on to back of apron

Cook's apron
Wear this apron to protect your clothes when you are cooking. Keep useful kitchen tools at hand in the apron pocket.

This pocket is divided in two by a line of stitching.

MARVELLOUS MOBILES

When it's raining outside and you are stuck indoors, why not make a new mobile for your room? Here you can find out how to make three brilliant mobiles from card or oven-hardening modelling clay, all using the same basic method. Copy the themes we have shown here, or design one of your own.

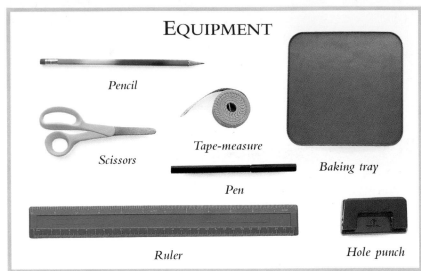

EQUIPMENT

Pencil

Scissors

Tape-measure

Baking tray

Pen

Ruler

Hole punch

You will need

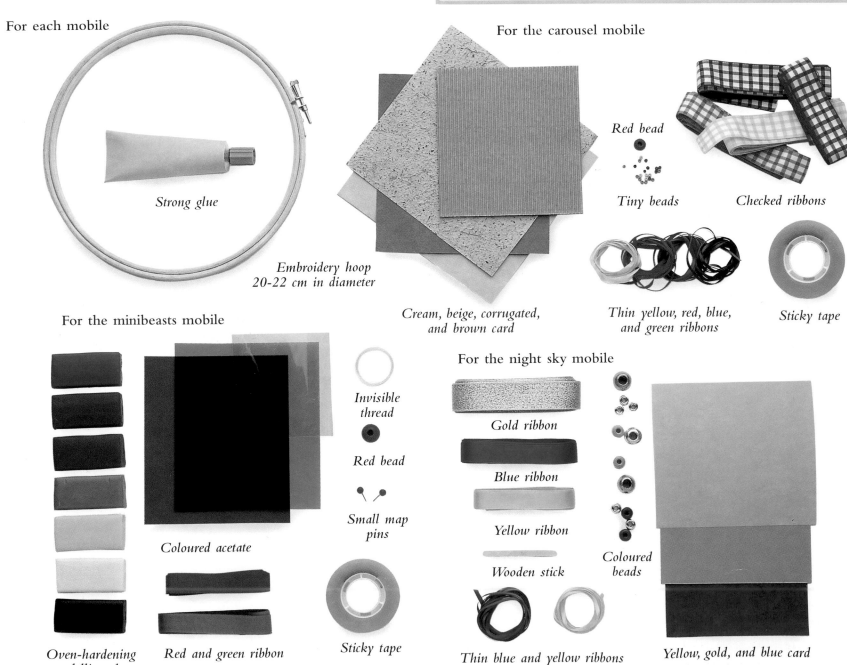

For each mobile

Strong glue

Embroidery hoop
20-22 cm in diameter

For the carousel mobile

Red bead

Tiny beads

Checked ribbons

Thin yellow, red, blue,
and green ribbons

Sticky tape

Cream, beige, corrugated,
and brown card

For the minibeasts mobile

Coloured acetate

Invisible
thread

Red bead

Small map
pins

For the night sky mobile

Gold ribbon

Blue ribbon

Yellow ribbon

Wooden stick

Coloured
beads

Oven-hardening
modelling clay

Red and green ribbon

Sticky tape

Thin blue and yellow ribbons

Yellow, gold, and blue card

Night sky mobile

1 Draw stars and moons on yellow, gold, and blue card and cut them out. For the centre of the mobile, draw and cut out a big quarter moon.

2 Punch a hole in each shape. Tie a thin ribbon through each hole and thread on a bead. Tie the moon to a wide ribbon 40 cm long.

3 Cover the embroidery hoop by wrapping blue and gold ribbon around it. Glue the ends of the ribbons in place to secure them.

Minibeasts mobile

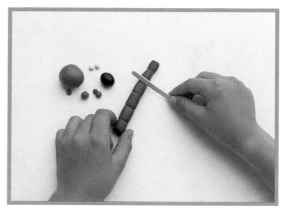

4 Cut four ribbons 30 cm long. Glue one end of each ribbon to the hoop. Thread the other ends and the moon's ribbon through a big bead.

5 Hold the mobile up to check that it hangs straight. Tie on the other stars and moon, checking that the mobile is still hanging straight.

1 Knead the clay and roll it into balls. Shape characters and leaves with different coloured clay. Use the stick to help you model the minibeasts.

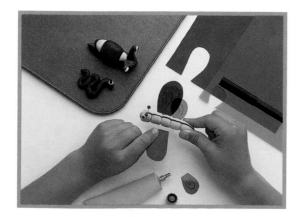

2 Put the minibeasts on a baking tray and harden them in the oven★. Allow to cool. For some insects, glue on coloured acetate wings.

3 Tie thread to each minibeast and check that it will hang straight. You may need to tie a thread to each end of the minibeast for balance.

4 Tape ribbons to the hoop, as above. Glue the clay leaves around the hoop for decoration. Hang the mobile up and tie on the minibeasts.

★Ask an adult to help you harden the clay. Always follow the instructions on the packet carefully.

MERRY-GO-ROUND!
Carousel mobile

1 Wrap checked ribbon around the hoop to cover it. Cut eight thin ribbons 90 cm long. Tie each one to the hoop, leaving 45 cm on one side.

2 Draw eight horse shapes on card and cut them out. Glue on the checked-ribbon saddles and the thin coloured-ribbon bridles and reins.

3 Thread the eight ribbons through a bead and check that the mobile hangs straight. Tape the other ends of the ribbons to the backs of the horses.

Displaying your mobile

Tie a loop in the ribbons above the bead and ask an adult to help you hang the mobile from the ceiling. Once it is up, you may have to adjust the position of some of the hanging objects so that the mobile balances well. For the best effect, hang the mobile where it will turn slowly in a breeze.

Fairground carousel
The finished mobile looks just like a fairground merry-go-round. For an added feeling of movement, trim the ribbons to different lengths and tape to the back of the horses.

Eight pieces of ribbon tied to the bound hoop balance the carousel.

Bead glued on for an eye

Bridles made of ribbon and beads

Ribbon taped to the back of the horse

Checked ribbon saddles

Corrugated card

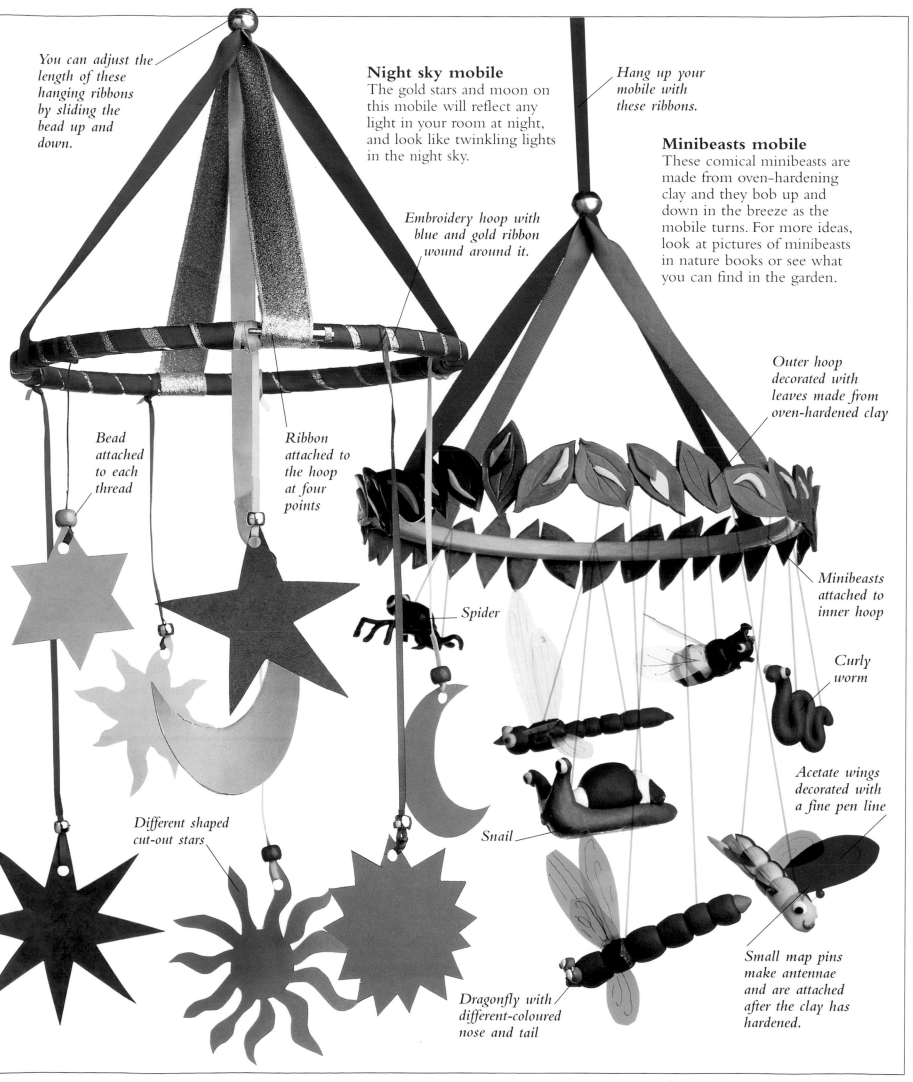

You can adjust the length of these hanging ribbons by sliding the bead up and down.

Night sky mobile
The gold stars and moon on this mobile will reflect any light in your room at night, and look like twinkling lights in the night sky.

Hang up your mobile with these ribbons.

Minibeasts mobile
These comical minibeasts are made from oven-hardening clay and they bob up and down in the breeze as the mobile turns. For more ideas, look at pictures of minibeasts in nature books or see what you can find in the garden.

Embroidery hoop with blue and gold ribbon wound around it.

Outer hoop decorated with leaves made from oven-hardened clay

Bead attached to each thread

Ribbon attached to the hoop at four points

Minibeasts attached to inner hoop

Spider

Curly worm

Acetate wings decorated with a fine pen line

Different shaped cut-out stars

Snail

Small map pins make antennae and are attached after the clay has hardened.

Dragonfly with different-coloured nose and tail

33

PAPER POTTERY

Papier mâché costs very little to make as it is made out of torn up newspaper. You can make the most amazing pottery with a few simple moulds. Here and over the page you can see how to create a golden treasure chest and bright plates and bowls for holding and displaying your treasures.

For the papier mâché

Old newspaper and white paper

PVA glue

You will need

For the treasure chest

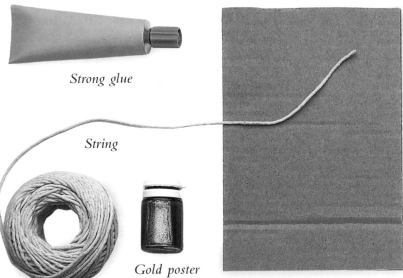

Strong glue

String

Gold poster paint

Corrugated card

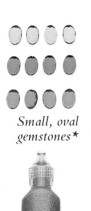

Glitter paint

Small, oval gemstones★

Large, round gemstones★

Sticky tape

Box with a lid

Making the plate

1 Tear newspaper into long strips and squares about 2 cm across. Mix PVA glue with a little water in a bowl and soak the paper in it.

2 Using the plate as a mould, cover the back with plastic wrap, then with six layers of glued paper. Make sure all the pieces of paper overlap.

3 Tear up some strips of white paper, soak them in the glue, and cover the plate with them. Leave the papier mâché to dry for a day.

★*Available from large department stores or craft shops.*

EQUIPMENT

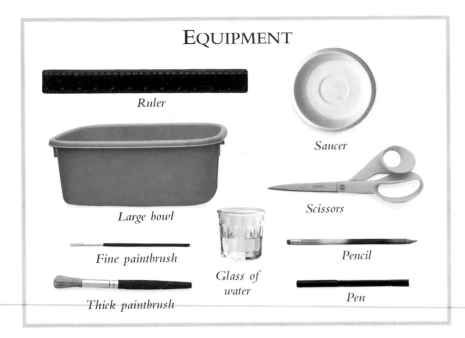

Ruler

Saucer

Scissors

Large bowl

Fine paintbrush

Pencil

Glass of water

Pen

Thick paintbrush

Gold and coloured tissue paper

For the plate and bowl

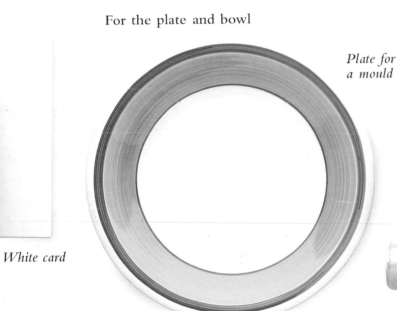

White card

Plate for a mould

Poster paints

Large bowl for a mould

Plastic wrap

Decorating the plate

4 Remove the mould. Cover the top of the paper plate with white paper soaked in glue. When it is dry, trim the edges of the plate.

Paste squares of coloured tissue paper on to the plate and gold tissue paper around the rim. Cover the bottom of the plate with gold tissue paper.

Painting the bowl

Make a bowl in the same way as the plate. Draw a pattern on the bowl, then paint it with poster paint. Paint the inside of the bowl gold.

POSTCARDS HOME

Home-made postcards are fun to make and your friends and family will treasure them as holiday memories. Choose a theme based on where you are spending your holiday – by the sea, in the country, or in a city – and remember to write an interesting message on the back.

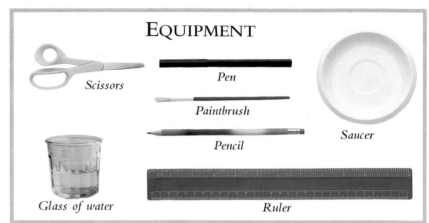

EQUIPMENT

Scissors

Pen

Paintbrush

Pencil

Saucer

Glass of water

Ruler

You will need

Plain and textured card and tracing paper

Coloured tissue paper

Blue cord

Glue stick

Small seashells

Strong glue

Poster paints

String

Making a postcard

1 Measure and cut out pieces of plain card the size you want your postcards. Carefully draw and then paint different pictures on them.

2 If you want to make a collage, cut out one of your paintings. Make a background on another card by gluing on torn pieces of paper.

3 Glue the painting to the background card. Carefully add any final details. Leave the back of the card blank to write your message.

Postcard gallery

All these cards have a seaside theme. Some are simply painted, some have cut-out shapes, and others are collages with different things stuck on them. If you are worried about a special postcard being damaged in the post, make an envelope for it out of thick paper.

This card has carefully been cut out in the shape of a crab.

Clawed crab

Flashing lighthouse

Bright yellow light

Black outline

Seashell collage

String glued in place

Torn tissue paper

Tasty ice cream

Seaside starfish

Seashell

Textured card

Swirls of thick paint

Cord tied around the edge

String border

Lifebuoy with a view

This card was cut out, then painted.

Space for address

The back of the card

Don't forget to leave the back of the card blank, with room for your message, the address the card is going to, and a stamp.

INDEX